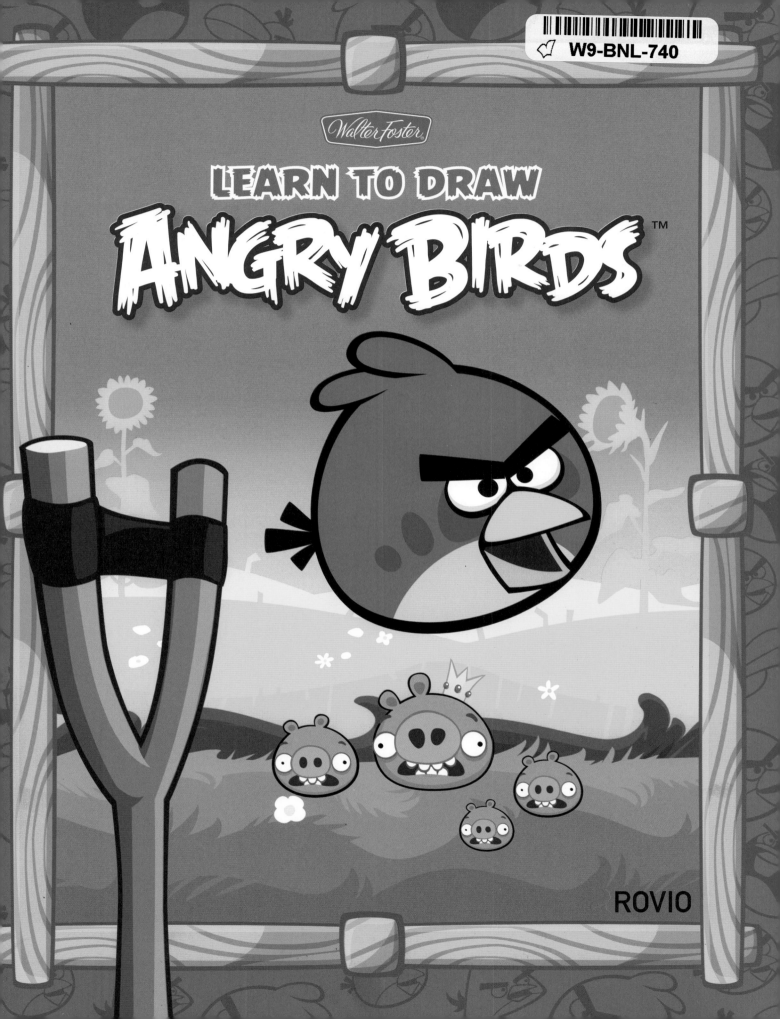

Step-by-step illustrations by Kristina Marroquin-Burr

3 5 7 9 10 8 6 4 2

TABLE OF CONTENTS

INTRODUCING THE ANGRY BIRDS

When greedy pigs steal the eggs, the Angry Birds set out on a mission to get the eggs back. Destroying the pigs' buildings by launching themselves as projectiles toward the structures, the Angry Birds use their special abilities to bring the pigs down and regain the eggs.

TOOLS & MATERIALS

Before you begin drawing, you will need to gather the right tools. Start with a regular pencil, an eraser, and a pencil sharpener. When you're finished with your drawing, you can bring your characters to life by adding color with crayons, colored pencils, markers, or even paint!

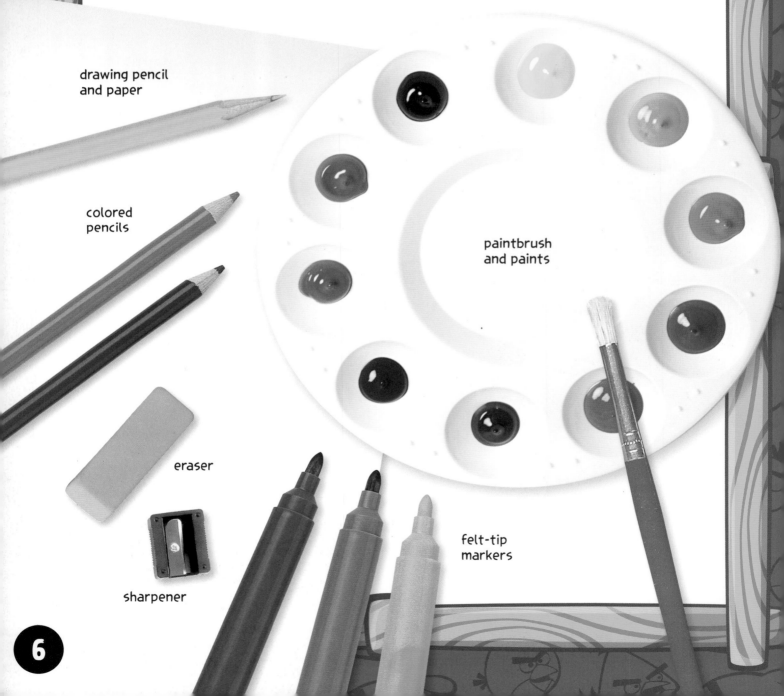

drawing pencil
and paper

colored
pencils

paintbrush
and paints

eraser

felt-tip
markers

sharpener

HOW TO USE THIS BOOK

Professional artists draw characters in steps. The key is to start with simple shapes and gradually add the details. The blue lines will help guide you through the process.

1 First you'll draw guidelines to help position the character's features.

2 Next, you'll add the details step by step.

3 When you finish adding the details, erase your guidelines. Then darken your final sketch lines with a pen or a marker.

I'm the Bomb!

SIZE CHART

Red   The Blues   Bubbles   Chuck   Hal

Minion Pig
Small

Minion Pig
Medium

Corporal Pig

Bomb

Matilda

Terence

Moustache Pig

King Pig

RED

Red is the iconic hero of Angry Birds and is instantly recognized everywhere in the world. The striking red plume and yellow beak of the fluffy Red bird really set him apart in a crowd.

RED'S EXPRESSIONS

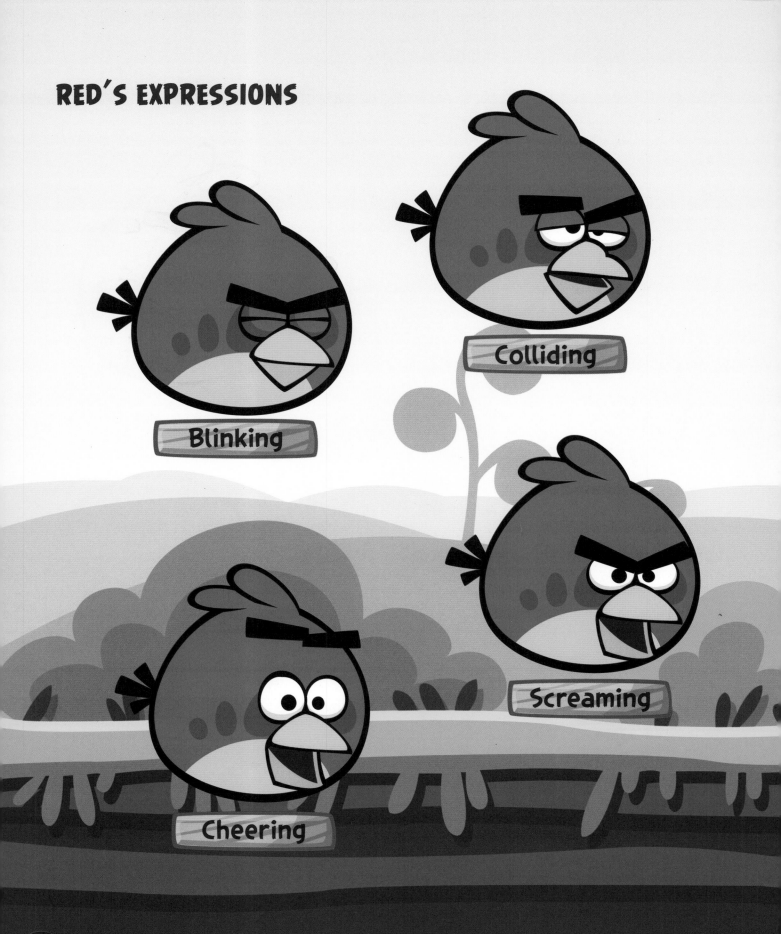

Blinking

Colliding

Cheering

Screaming

Flying

Jumping

Looking left

Looking right

TERENCE

Terence is bigger, wrinklier, and grumpier than Red. His only form of communication is staring. He is also very heavy.

1

2

3

CHUCK

Similar in size to Red, the almost cone-shaped Yellow bird, Chuck, speeds through the air like a bullet. The streamlined Yellow bird is slimmer than its Red brother.

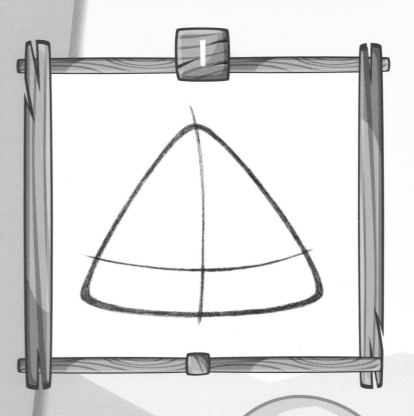

21

CHUCK'S EXPRESSIONS

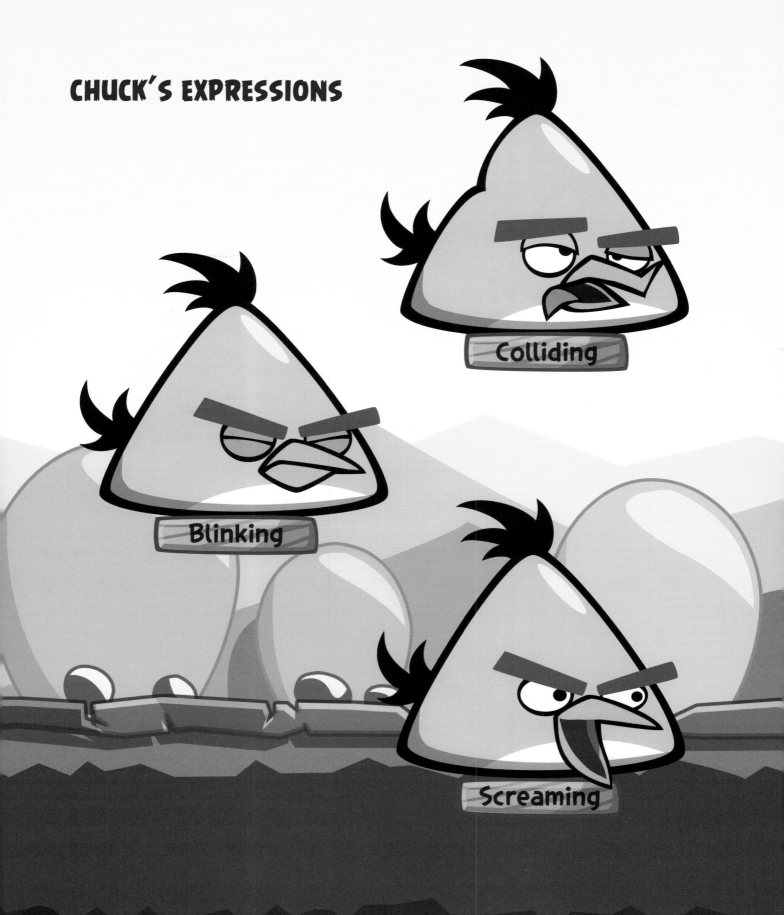

Colliding

Blinking

Screaming

Flying

Jumping

Looking left

BOMB

The exploding Bomb is the second largest bird. Bomb has a thin layer of jet-black feathers, which give him a shiny look, almost like a hard outer shell.

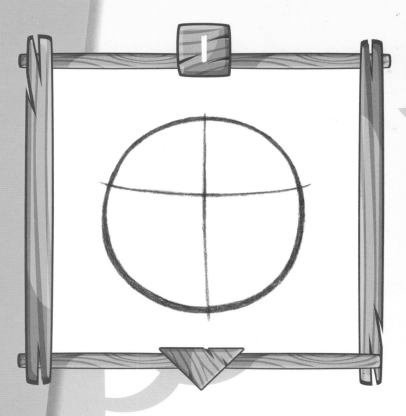

BOMB'S EXPRESSIONS

Blinking

Cheering

Colliding

Screaming

Flying

Jumping

Looking left

Looking right

MATILDA

Egg-laying Matilda sits between Red and Bomb in size. She has clean white feathers and a short, strong beak.

MATILDA'S EXPRESSIONS

Blinking

Cheering

Colliding

Screaming

Flying

Jumping

Deflated

Looking left

Looking right

37

HAL

Hal cannot be mistaken for any other bird, thanks to his massive, bright orange beak.

HAL'S EXPRESSIONS

Colliding

Blinking

Screaming

Cheering

Flying

Boomerang

Jumping

Looking left

THE BLUES

Jim, Jake & Jay travel in packs of three. While they don't share the characteristic eyebrows of the other Angry Birds, they are no less determined.

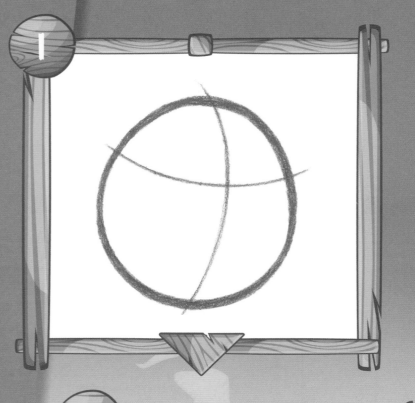

BUBBLES

Bubbles may look like the smallest of the bunch, but packs an exciting surprise. When threatened, Bubbles balloons up, pushing obstacles and enemies aside!

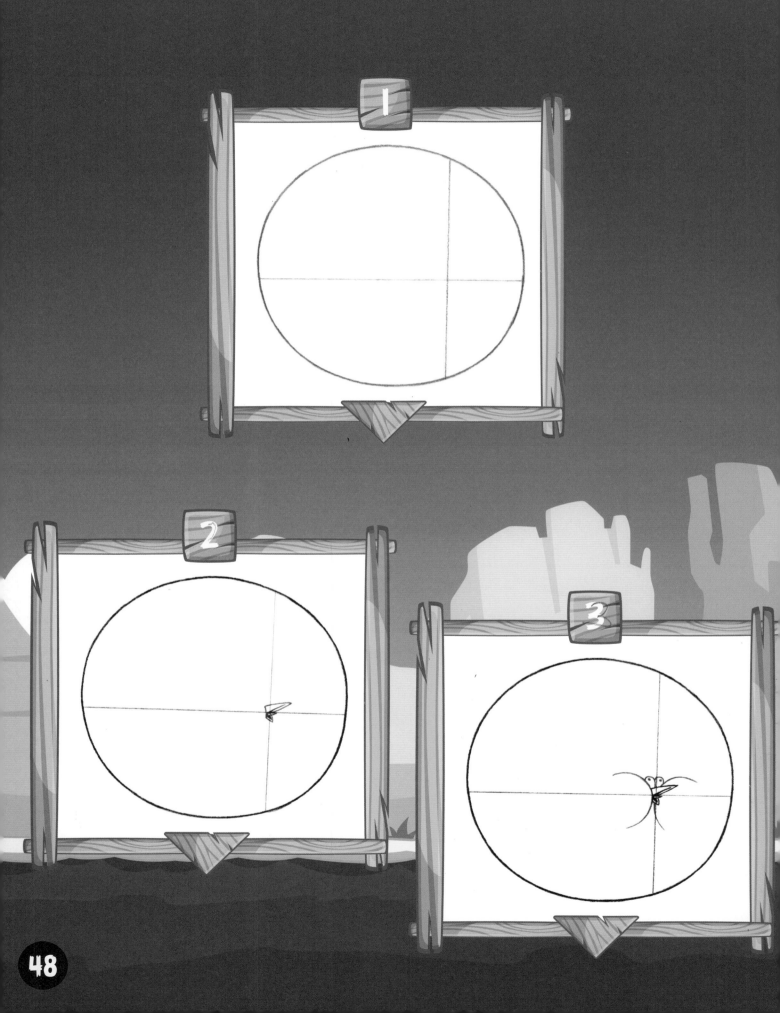

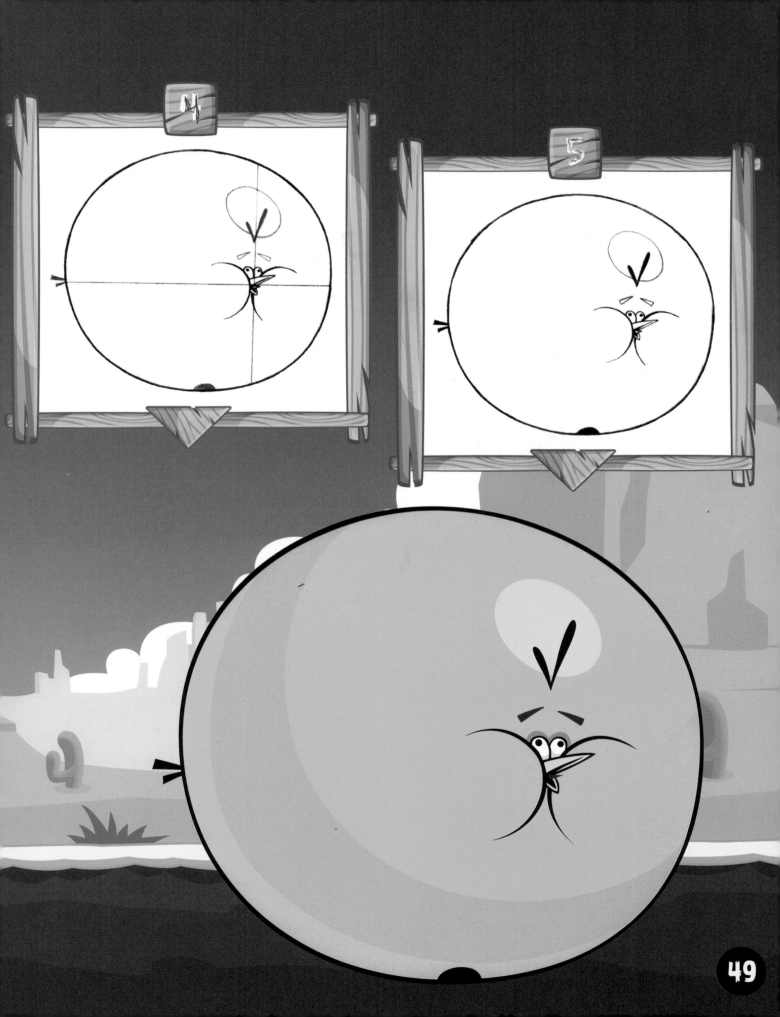

MINION PIGS

These cheeky creatures are Minion Pigs of the common egg-stealing variety. They are easily identified by their green skin; short and stubby snout; and their small, round ears.

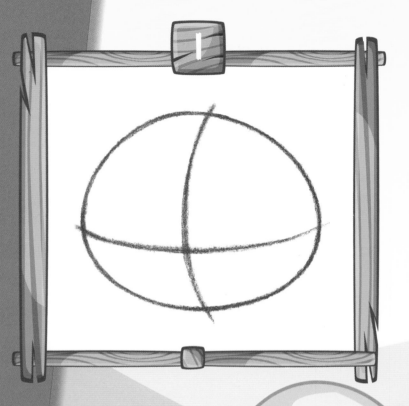

MINION PIGS' EXPRESSIONS

Damaged

Blinking

Scared

Laughing

Sad

Tongue out

Sleepy

Relieved

CORPORAL PIG

The Corporal Pig is a seasoned veteran and bulkier than the Minion Pigs. The Corporal Pig comes better prepared, and he wears a helmet of shining steel. However, under intense bird bombardment, even steel may bend, buckle, and crack!

1

2

3

MOUSTACHE PIG

The Moustache Pig is more senior than the Corporal Pig or the Minion Pigs. He is almost as large as the King Pig, but sits just below him in the pig hierarchy. Moustache Pig sports a bright orange moustache and matching eyebrows.

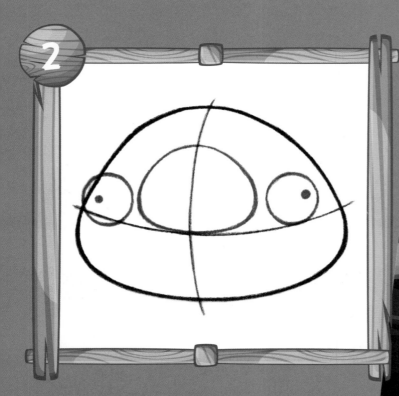

KING PIG

The King Pig is the ruler of all pigs. In addition to his bulk, he is identified from the common pigs by his shining golden crown, adorned with bright blue sapphires. The King Pig often opts for headgear appropriate to the climate and scenery—the various hats and helmets always have been the crown symbol of the boss.

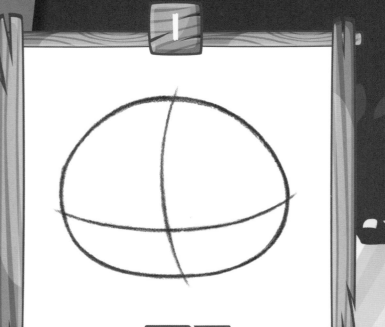

KING PIG'S EXPRESSIONS

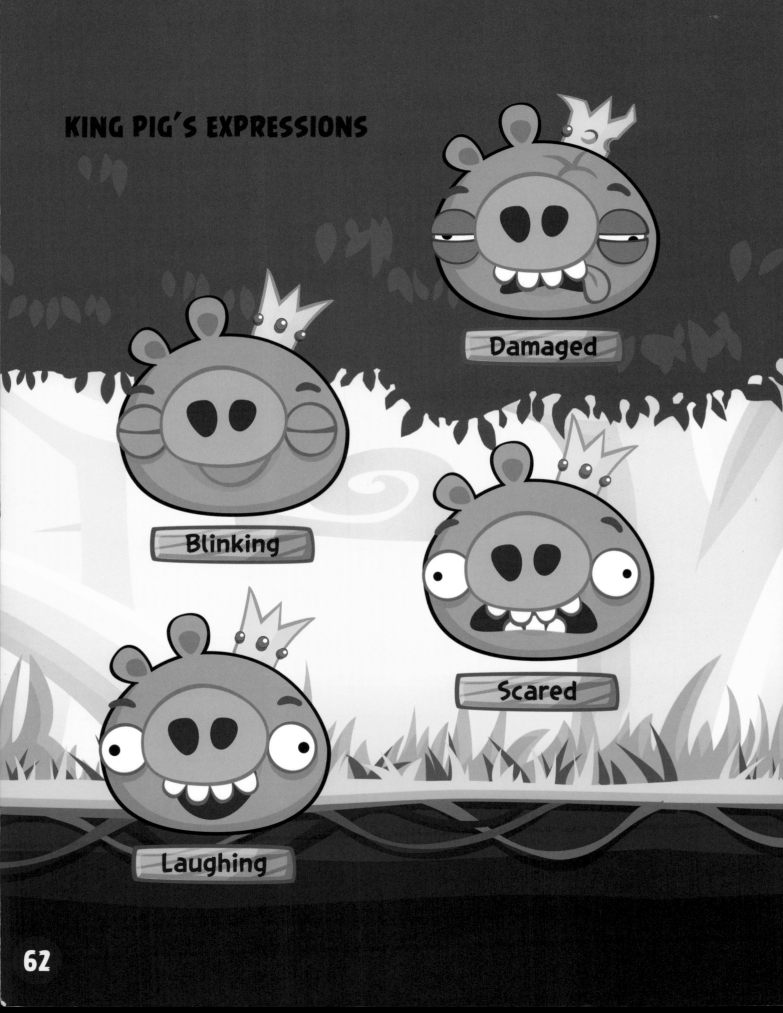

Damaged

Blinking

Scared

Laughing

Sad

Tongue out

Sleepy

Relieved

THE END

Now that you've learned the secrets to drawing the Angry Birds and their enemies, the Pigs, have fun re-creating your favorite levels from the popular game, or create your own! All you need is a pencil, paper, and your imagination!